LONDONTO▮▮▮ ▮ ▮ ▮
RHYMING SLANG HISTORY
AND DICTIONARY

COMPLETE GUIDE TO LONDON EAST END
COCKNEY DIALECT PHRASE BOOK

By
Jonathan Thomas

Anglotopia Press - An Imprint of Anglotopia LLC
www.anglotopia.press

Printed in the United States of America

1st US Edition: March 1st, 2023

Published by Anglotopia Press, an imprint of Anglotopia LLC.
The Anglotopia Press Name and Logo is a trademark of Anglotopia LLC.

Print Book interior design by Jonathan Thomas, all fonts used with license.

All location photographs © Jonathan Thomas
All other photos and art used in this book are in the public domain in the USA or in the Creative Commons.

Print ISBN: 978-1-955273-32-9

TABLE OF CONTENTS

INTRODUCTION

Londontopia's Cockney Rhyming Slang History and Dictionary is a comprehensive guide to one of the most unique and fascinating forms of language in the world. Cockney rhyming slang is a distinctive dialect that originated in the East End of London in the 19th century and has since become a symbol of working-class pride and cultural identity.

The most popular pages on Londontopia, our website dedicated to all things London, have always been the ones about Cockney. So, we thought it was a good time to compile the dozens of articles we have into a handy little book – and write some new articles as well just for this book!

This book is not just a dictionary of Cockney rhyming slang but also a journey through the history of London's East End, exploring the social and cultural context that gave rise to this distinctive dialect. From the rural villages of the 14th century to the densely populated urban area of the 18th and 19th centuries, the East End has always been a place of diversity, innovation, and creativity.

The book covers the origins of Cockney rhyming slang, including theories about its development as a secret code among criminals and underground groups in the East End. It also explores the cultural significance of the dialect, from its use as a way of distinguishing oneself from the upper classes to its celebration in popular culture through television shows, movies, and music.

Throughout the book, readers will discover a wealth of information about the unique language and culture of the East End. The dictionary itself includes hundreds of entries, covering everything from everyday words and phrases to more obscure and esoteric slang terms. Each entry is accompanied by a detailed explanation of its origins and meanings, as well as examples of how it might be used in context. Some experts will notice that many of the words are phrases are completely made up. You will not find two people who agree on what's made up. But that's how language is used and evolves – things get made up and then become the norm.

In addition to the dictionary, the book includes a range of other features that make it a must-read for anyone interested in Cockney rhyming slang or the history of London's East End. There are profiles of famous Cockneys, from musicians and actors to politicians and writers, as well as a guide to the best places to experience Cockney culture in London today.

Throughout the book, readers will also find fascinating insights into the social and cultural context of Cockney rhyming slang. For example, the book explores how the dialect was used as a way of asserting working-class identity in the face of poverty and hardship. It also looks at how the language has evolved over time and how it is still used today as a way of communicating among friends and family in the East End.

Perhaps most importantly, the book is written in a lively and engaging style that makes it accessible to readers of all ages and backgrounds. Whether you are a linguistics enthusiast, a fan of London history, or simply curious about the fascinating world of Cockney rhyming slang, this book is sure to provide hours of entertainment and education.

Londontopia's Cockney Rhyming Slang History and Dictionary is an essential resource for anyone interested in the unique language and culture of London's East End. Whether you are a native Londoner or a visitor to the city, this book will give you a deeper understanding and appreciation of one of the most distinctive and fascinating dialects in the world.

Jonathan Thomas
Publisher
Londontopia.net

WHAT IS A COCKNEY?

The term "cockney" is often used to describe someone from the East End of London. The term Cockney is also used as a demonym for a person from the East End or, traditionally, born within earshot of Bow Bells. The Bow Bells are the church bells at St Mary-le-Bow church in the East End of the City of London (more on that later).

The origins of the word are somewhat mysterious, but it is generally believed to have come from the Middle English word "cokenay," which meant a "cock's egg" or a "small, misshapen egg." Over time, the term came to be used to describe someone who was a bit of an oddball, or a "strange bird," as it were. But today, the term has come to be associated with a particular kind of Londoner with a distinctive accent and a certain set of cultural characteristics.

The history of the cockney can be traced back to the 14th century when the area now known as the East End of London was still largely rural. At that time, the area was home to a number of small villages and hamlets, which were populated by farmers, fishermen, and other rural workers. But as London grew, the East End began to change, and in the 18th and 19th centuries, it became a densely populated urban area, home to factories, warehouses, and slums.

It was during this time that the cockney accent began to emerge. The accent was a product of the diverse mix of people who were living in the East End at the time, including immigrants from Ireland, Scotland, and other parts of England. The accent was also influenced by the working-class culture of the East End, which was characterized by a strong sense of community and a certain rough-edged humor.

Over time, the cockney accent and the culture that it represented became a source of pride for many East Enders. The accent was seen as a way of distinguishing oneself from the more posh and refined accents of the upper classes, and the culture was seen as a way of asserting one's identity in the face of poverty and hardship.

One of the most famous aspects of cockney culture is the cockney rhyming slang. This is a form of slang in which a word is replaced by a phrase that rhymes with it. For example, "stairs" might be replaced by "apples and pears." The origins of this slang are unclear, but it is believed to have emerged in the 19th century as a way for criminals and other underworld figures to communicate without being understood by the police (this has been both discounted and proven, you decide).

Despite its origins in the East End, cockney

culture has spread throughout London and beyond. Today, the cockney accent and the associated culture are celebrated in films, television shows, and books, and there are even annual cockney festivals held in London.

However, the East End itself has undergone significant changes in recent years. Many of the old factories and warehouses have been converted into trendy apartments and offices, and the area is now home to a thriving arts scene and a number of upscale restaurants and bars. As a result, many East Enders feel that their traditional culture is being eroded, and there is a sense of nostalgia for the old days when the area was more working-class and rough around the edges. Many East Enders actually moved out of London after World War II during slum clearances (portrayed wonderfully in Call the Midwife), many to Essex, where the local accent shares many language and sound similarities (watch Gavin & Stacey for research).

A cockney is a distinctive kind of Londoner with a long and fascinating history. From its origins in the rural villages of the 14th century to its emergence as a symbol of working-class pride in the 19th and 20th centuries, the cockney has played an important role in the cultural life of London. While the East End itself may be changing, the spirit of the cockney lives on, and its accent and culture continue to be celebrated by people all over the world.

COCKNEY RHYMING SLANG HISTORY

Cockney rhyming slang is a unique and fascinating form of language that originated in London's East End in the 19th century. It is a form of slang that uses rhyming words or phrases to replace common words or phrases, often resulting in a completely different and often humorous meaning. For example, the phrase "apples and pears" is used to mean "stairs," while "trouble and strife" means "wife."

The origins of Cockney rhyming slang are somewhat unclear, but it is believed to have developed in the 1800s among the working-class communities in the East End of London. The East End was a melting pot of cultures and dialects, with immigrants from all over Europe coming to London to find work in the growing industrial city. The language they spoke was a mixture of English, Yiddish, and various other languages, and it was in this environment that cockney rhyming slang first emerged.

One theory about the origins of cockney rhyming slang is that it was developed as a secret code among criminals and other underground groups in the East End. The idea was that by using a language that only insiders could understand, they could communicate with each other without the police or other authorities being able to understand what they were saying. Another theory is that it was simply a way for people to have fun with language and create a sense of community among themselves.

Regardless of its origins, cockney rhyming slang quickly became popular among working-class Londoners, and it is still used today. It has even spread beyond London and has been adopted by people all over the world who find the language entertaining and unique.

One of the interesting things about cockney rhyming slang is that it is constantly evolving. New words and phrases are added all the time and old ones fall out of use. This means that the language is always changing and adapting to the times. There is no official authority on Cockney slang words; the words and phrases change and appear, usually in popular culture. Some fall out of use, while others are overused.

In addition to its use in everyday conversation, cockney rhyming slang has also been featured in movies, TV shows, and music. It has become a part of popular culture and is often used to add a touch of humor or authenticity to a piece of media set in London.

Overall, cockney rhyming slang is a fascinating and unique aspect of the English language. Its origins may be somewhat murky, but its impact on popular culture is clear. Whether you are a native Londoner or just a fan of language and linguistics, cockney rhyming slang is definitely worth exploring.

COMMON QUESTIONS ABOUT COCKNEY SLANG

What is Cockney Rhyming Slang?

Rhyming slang is usually composed of two nouns, which make an idiom, metaphor, or phrase in which the last word is intended to rhyme with the word that is actually meant. For example: "Slabs of Meat" means feet. However, in many cases, the rhyming words are removed, making it difficult for anyone who doesn't know the rhyme to know exactly what is going on. Another example is "Oh, my slabs don't half hurt," meaning "my feet hurt."

What is a Cockney?

The true meaning of "Cockney" was used to describe someone born within the radius that can hear the bells of Mary-le-Bow church in Cheapside, London. Nowadays, it applies to most London-born folk, especially in the suburbs and outer London boroughs, as they still have the Cockney accent. It is rarely heard in Central London.

Is Cockney Rhyming a Thing of the Past?

No, quite the opposite. It still lives in today's spoken language and is not only limited to the London area. Much of the UK understands and often uses rhyming slang in their day-to-day conversations.

Is Cockney Rhyming Slang Evolving?

There is no doubt that Cockney rhyming slang is constantly evolving and developing. It changes to incorporate modern pop culture icons into their rhyming schemes, such as Ayton Senna–Tenner, a £10 note. It has also evolved to incorporate new modern-day terminology, such as "Wind and Kite," as rhyming slang for Website.

Examples

Here are some examples for you to try out yourself. The format is "Rhyme," "Meaning," and "What people actually say."

Slabs of Meat – Feet – Slabs

Mince Pies – Eyes – Mincers

Old China Plate – Mate – China or Ol' China

Apples & Pears – Stairs – Apples

Dog & Bone – Phone – Dog

Trouble and Strife – Wife – Trouble

Bangers & Mash – Cash – Bangers

Bees & Honey – Money- Honey

You are now set for a visit to London and be able to fit in with the locals. Don't be shy and happily shout your newly learned phrases at the top of your voice. We are sure the neighbors will love it. You can walk around London having a clear "Scooby Doo" (clue) about what is going on.

Actually, don't do any of that. Any attempts by Americans or foreigners to talk like a Cockney will be met with derision and ridicule!

A HISTORY OF ST MARY-LE-BOW CHURCH

THE COCKNEY CATHEDRAL

St. Mary-le-Bow church, located in the heart of the City of London, has a rich history dating back centuries. Its connection to London Cockneys is significant, as it is traditionally considered the spiritual home of the true Cockney, and its association with the iconic Bow Bells has become deeply ingrained in London folklore.

The history of St. Mary-le-Bow can be traced back to the Norman Conquest of England in 1066. The original church was destroyed in the Great Fire of London in 1666 and was subsequently rebuilt by Sir Christopher Wren, who designed many of the city's iconic structures after the devastating fire (you can tell what a Wren church looks like by looking at it!). The new St. Mary-le-Bow was completed in 1680 and has since stood as a symbol of resilience and architectural beauty in the heart of the bustling metropolis.

One of the most distinctive features of St. Mary-le-Bow is its set of bells, commonly referred to as the Bow Bells. These bells have played a crucial role in the church's connection to Cockney culture. According to tradition, a true Cockney is someone born within the sound of the Bow Bells. This has given rise to the popular saying "as true as the Bow Bells," signifying the authenticity of someone's London roots.

The association between St. Mary-le-Bow and Cockneys is not merely geographical; it is deeply rooted in the social and cultural history of London. Cockneys, often characterized by their distinctive accent and unique slang, have long been considered a quintessential part of London's identity. The connection to

St. Mary-le-Bow adds a spiritual dimension to this identity, as the church becomes a symbol of the cultural heritage of those born in the East End of London.

Over the centuries, St. Mary-le-Bow has witnessed the ebb and flow of London's history. From royal ceremonies to wartime destruction, the church has stood as a silent witness to the changing fortunes of the city. Its resilience in the face of challenges reflects the enduring spirit of London itself.

During World War II, St. Mary-le-Bow suffered significant damage during the Blitz, a series of German air raids targeting London from 1940 to 1941. The church's iconic steeple was destroyed, but efforts were made to rebuild and restore it to its former glory in the post-war years. The restoration process not only preserved the physical structure of St. Mary-le-Bow but also reinforced its cultural and historical significance.

In addition to its role in Cockney folklore, St. Mary-le-Bow has been a center of religious and community life for centuries. Its interior is adorned with beautiful stained-glass windows, intricate carvings, and a sense of serenity that contrasts with the bustling city outside its doors. The church has hosted countless weddings, christenings, and funerals, marking the milestones of generations of Londoners.

The connection between St. Mary-le-Bow and London Cockneys goes beyond the geographical and linguistic. It embodies a sense of belonging and continuity, linking past and present generations of Londoners. The Bow Bells, with their distinctive chime, serve as a constant reminder of the city's rich history and the resilient spirit of its people.

As London continues to evolve and embrace its multicultural identity, St. Mary-le-Bow remains a touchstone for those who cherish the traditions and stories that have shaped the city. The church stands as a living testament to the enduring bond between London and its Cockney inhabitants, a bond that transcends time and continues to resonate in the vibrant tapestry of urban life.

COCKNEY FILMS AND TV SHOWS

Cockney culture has long been a staple in British film and television. From gritty crime dramas set in London's East End to heartwarming musicals, the influence of Cockney culture on British entertainment cannot be denied. In this chapter, we will take a trip down memory lane and look at the top Cockney films and TV shows that have captivated audiences throughout history. From the classic "Lock, Stock and Two Smoking Barrels" to the beloved "EastEnders" and everything in between, get ready to explore the best of what this unique and vibrant culture has to offer.

And yes, quite a few of these films will have been directed by Guy Ritchie…

RocknRolla (2008) - "RocknRolla" is a crime-comedy film set in London, featuring a group of criminals who get caught up in a real estate deal gone wrong. It was released in 2008 and directed by Guy Ritchie.

Lock, Stock and Two Smoking Barrels (1998) is a comedy-crime film set in London's East End, featuring a group of young men who get mixed up in a high-stakes card game.

EastEnders (1985-present) - A long-running British soap opera set in the fictional London borough of Walford, following the lives of working-class families and their struggles.

Snatch (2000) is a crime-comedy film set in London featuring a group of criminals who get caught up in a stolen diamond heist.

The Krays (1990) is a biographical film about the notorious Kray twins, who were gangsters in the East End of London in the 1960s.

Legend (2015) is another biographical film about the Kray brothers, this one starring Tom Hardy as both brothers.

Only Fools and Horses (1981-2003) - A British sitcom about a group of working-class characters living in Peckham, South London, and their various schemes to make money.

Mary Poppins (1964) is a musical fantasy film set in Edwardian London about a magical nanny who brings joy and order to the Banks family. Dick Van Dyke famous played a Cockney chimney sweep, but heavy on the stereotypes.

My Fair Lady (1964) is a musical film about a Cockney flower girl who is transformed into a proper lady by a phonetics professor.

Oliver Twist (1968) is a film adaptation

of Charles Dickens's classic novel set in Victorian London. It features the story of a young orphan boy who falls in with a gang of pickpockets.

Green Street (2005) - A sports drama film set in London, featuring the world of football hooliganism and the rivalry between West Ham United and Millwall fans.

RocknRolla (2008) is a crime-comedy film set in London featuring a group of criminals who get caught up in a real estate deal gone wrong.

Alfie (1966) is a romantic comedy-drama film about a Cockney playboy who pursues various women in swinging 1960s London.

Made in Dagenham (2010) - A film based on the true story of female factory workers in Dagenham, East London, who went on strike for equal pay in 1968.

The Long Good Friday (1980) - A crime thriller film set in London featuring a gangster who tries to keep his criminal empire intact while dealing with various threats.

Quadrophenia (1979) - A film about the mod subculture in the 1960s, set in London and featuring a young man who gets caught up in violence and rebellion.

Bronson (2008) is a biographical film about the notorious British criminal Charles Bronson, who spent most of his life in prison.

The Sweeney (2012) - A crime film based on the 1970s British TV series of the same name, featuring a team of London police officers who use unorthodox methods to catch criminals.

An American Werewolf in London (1981) - A horror-comedy film about two American tourists who are attacked by a werewolf in London.

Fish Tank (2009) is a drama film about a teenage girl living on a council estate in Essex who dreams of becoming a dancer.

Goodbye, Mr. Chips (1969) is a film

adaptation of the classic novel set in a boys' boarding school in England. It features the story of a beloved teacher.

The Ladykillers (1955) - A classic British comedy film about a group of criminals who rent a room in an old lady's house and plan a robbery.

The Italian Job (1969) - A classic British heist film set in Turin, Italy, featuring a group of criminals who plan to steal gold from a bank.

The Inbetweeners (2008-2010) - A British sitcom about four teenage boys growing up in suburbia, featuring their various misadventures and attempts to be cool.

Withnail and I (1987) - A comedy-drama film about two unemployed actors in 1960s London who go on a drunken holiday to the countryside.

The Bill (1984-2010) is a long-running British police procedural TV series set in London featuring the officers of Sun Hill police station.

Mr. Bean (1990-1995) is a British comedy TV series featuring the misadventures of the titular character, a bumbling man-child played by Rowan Atkinson, living in London.

GREAT LONDON TELLY: A BRIEF HISTORY OF EASTENDERS

EastEnders is a British television institution that has had a significant impact on the country's cultural landscape since its debut in 1985. The show, set in the fictional London borough of Walford, has become a household name and a mainstay of British television with its gritty portrayal of working-class life, diverse cast, and willingness to tackle difficult social issues. Over the years, EastEnders has captured the hearts of millions of viewers and has left an indelible mark on British television. It has even found an audience outside of the UK and remains popular in the USA and other former British colonies.

Key Facts

- EastEnders is the longest-running soap opera on BBC television, having first aired on February 19, 1985.
- The show has had over 6,000 episodes, and its 35th-anniversary episode, which aired in February 2020, was a live one.
- The "Who Shot Phil?" storyline in 2001 drew in an audience of over 22 million viewers, making it one of the most-watched television episodes in British history.
- Over the years, EastEnders has won numerous awards, including seven BAFTAs and 14 National Television Awards.
- The show has introduced several iconic characters over the years, including Dot Cotton, Peggy Mitchell, and Pat Butcher, who have become household names in the UK.

A Brief History

EastEnders is a British soap opera that first aired on the BBC in 1985 and has since become one of the most popular and influential TV shows in the country. Set in the fictional east London borough of Walford, the show follows the lives of a diverse group of characters and has tackled numerous social issues over the years.

The show was created by Julia Smith and Tony Holland and was originally intended to be a rival to the long-running ITV soap Coronation Street. However, EastEnders quickly established itself as a force to be reckoned with, thanks to its gritty, realistic portrayal of life in a working-class London community.

Right from the start, EastEnders was known for its controversial storylines and its willingness to tackle taboo subjects. In the early years, the show dealt with issues such as domestic violence, teenage pregnancy, and racism and was praised for its willingness to address these topics head-on.

Perhaps the most famous storyline in the show's history was the "Who Shot Phil?" plot, which saw one of the show's most popular characters, Phil Mitchell, left for dead after being shot. The mystery surrounding the identity of the shooter kept viewers on the edge of their seats for months, and the reveal episode was watched by over 22 million people.

Over the years, EastEnders has continued to push boundaries and tackle difficult issues. In recent years, the show has dealt with subjects such as mental health, homelessness, and knife crime and has been praised for its sensitive and nuanced approach to these topics.

But it's not just the show's controversial storylines that have made it such an important part of British culture. EastEnders has also been praised for its diverse cast, which has included actors from a wide range of ethnic and cultural backgrounds. This diversity has helped to make the show more representative of modern Britain and has given a platform to actors who might otherwise struggle to find work in the entertainment industry.

Another key factor in the show's success has been its ability to capture the spirit of its setting. The fictional borough of Walford is based on the real-life East End of London, and the show's creators have always been careful to depict the area's people and culture accurately. From the local pubs to the market stalls, EastEnders has always felt like an authentic portrayal of life in this part of the city.

Stars Who Got Their Start

EastEnders has been a breeding ground for some of the biggest names in British film and television. Over the years, the show has served as a launching pad for many aspiring actors, giving them a platform to showcase their talents and kick-start their careers.

One of the most famous examples is Dame Barbara Windsor, who played the iconic character of Peggy Mitchell on the show. Windsor went on to have a successful career in film and television, appearing in productions such as the Carry-On films and the BBC sitcom Dad's Army. Other notable

EastEnders alumni include Ross Kemp, who played the hardman Grant Mitchell, and Letitia Dean, who played the feisty Sharon Watts. Both Kemp and Dean have gone on to have successful careers in British television, with Kemp hosting documentaries and Dean appearing in shows such as Casualty and Doctors.

Cultural Impact

Perhaps the most important legacy of EastEnders is the way it has brought important social issues into the mainstream. By tackling subjects such as racism, domestic violence, and mental health, the show has helped to raise awareness of these issues and start important conversations. It has also provided a platform for charities and organizations working in these areas to reach a wider audience and has helped to break down some of the stigma surrounding these topics.

It is said that so many people watch EastEnders every day that Britain's electrical grid has to be managed closely before and after it starts, as the entire nation of viewers will switch on their tea kettles at the same time.

EastEnders is much more than just a TV show. It is a cultural institution that has shaped the way we think about the working-class communities of London and has helped to raise awareness of important social issues. From its controversial storylines to its diverse cast, the show has always been at the forefront of British culture and will no doubt continue to be for many years to come.

Places to Visit

You can get a flavor of the East End by visiting London and going on an EastEnders-related tour. The BBC does not currently offer tours of the sets (but they may in the future as Coronation Street, a competing soap, does tours).

There are plenty of places you can visit in London to get a taste of the show's setting. One of the most iconic locations is the Queen Vic pub, which has been a fixture on the show since its early days. The exterior of the pub is located in the real-life East End neighborhood of Wapping, and fans can visit for a pint and a photo opportunity. Another must-visit location is the Bridge Street market, which has appeared on the show for many years. Located in the real-life neighborhood of Bridge Street, the market is a great place to pick up some fresh produce and soak up the local atmosphere. Other locations worth visiting include the Beale house, the Mitchell house, and the Arches garage, all of which have been featured prominently on the show over the years.

Further Research

- "EastEnders: 20 Years In Albert Square" by Rupert Smith
- "The EastEnders Handbook" by Hilary Kingsley
- "EastEnders: The Inside Story" by Emily Herbert
- "EastEnders Who's Who" by Kate Lock
- "EastEnders: The First 10 Years" by Colin Brake
- "EastEnders: The Inside Story" by Julia Smith and Tony Holland

- "EastEnders: The Unofficial Companion" by Tony Holland and Julia Smith
- "EastEnders: The Inside Story" by Sharon Marshall
- "EastEnders: The Official Handbook" by David Stafford
- "The EastEnders Family Album" by Hilary Kingsley.

Where to Watch

You can stream the 'new' episodes of EastEnders on the BritBox streaming service. You cannot stream old episodes of Eastenders in the USA. The BBC iPlayer, which is only accessible within the UK, has old episodes.

GREAT LONDON TELLY: ONLY FOOLS AND HORSES

O nly fools and horses work for a living' was the obscure expression the working-class writer John Sullivan chose for the title. His sitcom follows the ups and downs of an illegal street trader, Del Boy, his younger brother, and Grandad, as they attempt to escape from both poverty and class, a hopeless task on both counts, although, in the end, wealth proves easier to achieve than entry in the higher classes of English society. Del's many 'get rich quick' schemes provide endless comic opportunities, and Sullivan's finely observed characters grow and evolve as the seasons flow by, with the ups and downs of real life seen through a satirical and comic lens.

Key Facts:

- Six seasons were shown between 1981 and 1999, plus specials
- Starred David Jason as Derek' Del Boy' Trotter, Nicholas Lyndhurst as Rodney Trotter, and Lennard Pierce as Grandad
- Voted Britain's Best Sitcom in 2004
- Written by John Sullivan, who grew up in working-class Balham
- Developed a strong cult following and contributed to English slang

A Short History

Although locked into a complex class structure, the British are still able to laugh equally at the foibles of all its social groups. Shows like 'Steptoe & Son' and 'Till Death us do Part' in the 1960s aimed at the working class, while the later 'Spitting Image' skewered Royalty with a sharp spear. The foibles of the working class, though, have always been a rich source for comedy writers, and the appeal of the social faux pas for comic effect is always tempting. The bustling street markets of London and the eccentricities of the street traders were the inspiration for Only Fools and Horses, a TV comedy series that ran throughout the 1980s and was voted 'Britain's Best Sitcom' in 2004.

Only Fools and Horses follows the daily life of market trader Derek 'Del Boy' Trotter, his younger brother Rodney, and their Grandad as they struggle to find the wealth to escape their life in Peckham, a working-class neighborhood of south-east London. They live in a council flat (state-provided and owned apartment) in Nelson Mandala House, a grim high-rise apartment building, and ever since their mother died when the boys were young, and their father left shortly afterward, Derek has been the family head and provider, surviving by buying and selling odd items that may have 'fallen off the back of a truck' or have come his way under other doubtful circumstances. His goal is to become a millionaire with some dubious scheme or other, and these plans – always unsuccessful – form the basis of the plots, which usually occupy a single episode. Only later in the series did longer story arcs begin, and a broader picture of their lives and surrounding society emerged. By the end of the series, a viewer has gained a rich picture of the backstories of the characters, and this 'epic novel' character of the show is a secondary strength to its immediate comedy.

The accuracy of the characters is guaranteed since the writer, John Sullivan, grew up in Balham, another south London working-class area. His father was a plumber, and he remembers always being fascinated by the bottom end of the street market scene and particularly the men variously called: 'spivs'; 'fly traders' (because they traded 'on the fly' to dodge the authorities); or, later, 'readies' (ready for anything). Often selling out of suitcases they opened on the street, these characters were Sullivan's inspiration for Derek Trotter. Sullivan had left school unqualified and eked out a living as a young man in a variety of unskilled jobs, from messenger boy to window cleaner and carpet layer. He persisted in submitting scripts to the BBC, finding his first success with Citizen Smith, and then being commissioned to create Only Fools and Horses.

The show was first aired on the 8th of September 1981, and the first season ran for six episodes, each of 30 minutes. Further seasons, usually also of 6 episodes, ran in 1982, 1983, 1985, 1986, 1989, and 1990. In addition, almost every year, there was a Christmas Special episode, and in 1996, three one-hour episodes ran as a Christmas Trilogy. Each Christmas Day of 2001, 2002, and 2003, an additional 75-minute specials were shown. A variety of sketches, promotional pieces, and other shorts were created between 1992 and 2015.

The story arc follows 'Del Boy' (played by David Jason) in his cheap gold jewelry and camel coat as he strives to become rich, eventually achieving that and then losing most of it again. His business, Trotters Independent Traders (T.I.T.), operates out of a suitcase or from the back of his yellow three-wheel van. By the end of the series, he has begun to emulate the richer 'yuppies' who are gentrifying his neighborhood.

After a succession of failed relationships, he eventually meets his 'significant other' in a late episode. Rodney typifies the working-class man who struggles to present himself as 'classier' – an effort always doomed to failure in a society with an acute ear for the subtle cues of class. He affects knowledge he lacks, in particular by attempting to use basic French, but always wrongly. When on holiday in Spain (a stereotypical working-class destination), he takes a 'fiesta' after lunch. Much of the humor in the series lies in the knowing way an English person will see through these ultimately pathetic attempts to be what he is not.

Rodney (played by Nicholas Lyndhurst) struggles to free himself from Derek's control and looks scornfully at the shady ways Derek tries to become rich. Rodney did well in school but was expelled from Art College for smoking cannabis and now struggles to become independent. He finds himself a middle-class girlfriend, Cassandra (played by Gwyneth Strong), who lives on the fashionable King's Road. Even though he lies about his background, she takes to him, and their relationship and marriage continue through the later seasons.

The foil to the younger generations is Grandad (played by Lennard Pierce), who is a stereotypical infirm 'OAP' – old age pensioner – who watches TV all day and is generally abused and derided by his grandchildren. When Pierce died in 1984, Grandad was buried, and his place was taken by Uncle Albert (played by Buster Merryfield), who can always be relied upon for a story that begins, "During the war..." When Merryfield died in 1999, his character also died, and his ashes were scattered in the English Channel. By the sixth series, the writer wanted Del Boy to give up chasing younger girls and settle down, so he created Racquel (played by Tessa Peake-Jones), a woman Del meets through a dating agency. Kind-hearted like Del, but also a failure, she has tried to be an actress but more often works as a stripagram. By the end of the series, they are still not married, although Del seems interested in settling down.

Minor characters in the series include Trigger (Roger Lloyd-Pack and Lewis Osborne), who is a street sweeper and not too bright. He is a regular at the local pub, the Nags Head, and his father "Died a few years before he was born." Boycie (John Challis) is a successful used-car salesman and the richest man at the Nag's Head, while Denzil (Paul Barber) is a long-distance lorry driver and regular victim of Del's get-rich schemes. The crooked policeman, DCI Slater (Jim Broadbent), only appears in three episodes but is a regular presence in the background of the series.

Cultural Impact

Initial viewing figures for the show were well below 10 million, but by the end of the third series, that barrier had been broken, and it eventually peaked at 24.3 million for the third episode of the 1996 Christmas trilogy – over 40% of the national population at the time. After it was voted Britain's Best Sitcom in 2004, several 'Story of. . .' documentaries were produced. Two spin-off series, The

Green, Green Grass, and Rock & Chips, were produced in the early 21st century, and a stage-play version was launched in February 2019 at the Theatre Royal Haymarket, London. Two board games based on the show were also created. The show has also won numerous popularity awards, and it ranks high in polls of the greatest TV shows ever.

The show has been viewed internationally, with particular interest in the countries of the former Yugoslavia, where the show is called Mućke, meaning 'shady deals.' It was remade in The Netherlands as Wat schuift't? (What's it worth?), and in Portugal and Slovenia. Several attempts to launch a US remake have been made, only to be rejected in their final stages.

The 'Only Fools and Horses Appreciation Society' was launched in 1993 with around 7,000 members. It releases a quarterly newsletter, and it has annual conventions of fans and cast members. It also stages Shows featuring props from the show, such as the yellow van.

Several of the tag lines from the series have entered everyday speech in England, such as 'Plonker' (a fool or idiot), 'Cushty' (good, delightful), and 'Lovely jubbly.' The show has reinforced cultural stereotypes of working-class people and habits, as well as disarming them by turning those elements into comedy memes.

Places to Visit

- London still has many street markets, but most have been gentrified in various ways and may give only a limited picture of the flavor of traditional markets.
- Deptford Market is near 'Del territory,' and this basic market of food and cheap goods runs from 7 am to 4 pm, Wednesday, Friday, and Saturday, on Deptford High Street.
- Brick Lane Market is held on Sundays from 9 am to 5 pm, and it has a range of goods. This traditional east-end market has gone upscale to a degree and today incorporates the nearby Truman Market.
- Petticoat Lane Market operates every

weekday and Sunday morning. It is primarily a clothing market with much of the old atmosphere. It is situated in Spitalfields, near Aldgate Tube Station. A Sunday visit could include the nearby Columbia Road Flower Market.

- Although set in Peckham, most of the show, and all the later series, were filmed in Bristol. Several small companies offer tours of outdoor locations.

- Tower blocks in the UK have gone from being desirable council housing when first built in the 1950s to scenes of social decay and back to desirable housing again today, in private hands. Towers such as Trellick Tower (Kensal Town), Keeling House (Bethnal Green), Sivill House (Shoreditch), and The Barbican Estate (City of London) are admired and desirable homes for young professionals in particular. Many are iconic, listed buildings and examples of British brutalist architecture. A visit is a reminder that there is more to Britain than ancient buildings and museums.

Where to Watch

- Complete collections of all the series of 'Only Fools and Horses' are available on DVD.
- Netflix is currently not steaming the series, but it is available on Britbox.
- All episodes of the show are available for download purchase on iTunes.

Further Research

- "The Only Fools and Horses Story, by Steve Clark, 1996
- "The Complete A-Z of Only Fools and Horses, by Richard Weber, 2003
- The Bible of Peckham. a three-volume edition of all the scripts, 2017
- He Who Dares…, by Jim Sullivan, a fictional autobiography of Derek Trotter, 2015
- You Know It Makes Sense, Lessons from The Derek Trotter School of Business (And Life), by Jim Sullivan, 2018
- The People: The Rise and Fall of the Working Class, 1910-2010, by Selina

Todd
- The Myth of Meritocracy: Why Working-Class Kids Still Get Working-Class Jobs, by James Bloodworth

LONDON'S PEARLY KINGS AND QUEENS

L ondon's Pearly Kings and Queens are a beloved institution that has been part of the city's cultural landscape for well over a century. These flamboyantly dressed individuals are instantly recognizable with their suits, jackets, and hats adorned with thousands of mother-of-pearl buttons, all sewn on by hand. Their tradition of charitable work and fundraising has been an important part of London life for generations, and their unique style and commitment to their communities have made them a treasured part of the city's identity. In this chapter, we'll explore the fascinating history of the Pearly Kings and Queens and the important role they have played in London's cultural heritage.

The Pearly Kings and Queens were started by Henry Croft in 1875. Croft was an orphan born in a St. Pancras workhouse and raised in an orphanage in Somers Town, London, which he left at the age of 13 to start making his own way in the world. His first job was as a municipal street sweeper, and this brought him into contact with the "Costers" or "Costermongers," street traders who wore pearl buttons sewn into the seams of their clothes. In a tight-knit community, the Costers would look after each other if one was sick or in need, and Croft became very enamored of their lifestyle.

Inspired by the Costermongers, Croft made himself a suit covered in pearl buttons and used it to aid his fundraising for charity. Henry collected the pearls that had fallen off of others' suits, and since he had no one to sew on the mother-of-pearl buttons for him, he learned how to do it himself. This started the tradition that Pearlies designed and sewed their own pearly suits. Eventually, Croft had collected enough buttons that his suit was covered in them and has since become known as a "smothered" suit. As the need for his charity work grew, he turned to the Costmongers to help him, with some of them becoming the first Pearly families.

By 1911, each of London's 28 metropolitan boroughs had its own Pearly King, Pearly Queen, and Pearly families. When Croft died in 1930 at age sixty-eight, his funeral train was half a mile long and comprised 400 Pearly Kings and Queens and people from the charities that he helped. The families passed on their traditions to their children, including both the construction of the pearly suits and the design symbols and their meanings.

In addition to the "smothered" suit made famous by Croft, the more well-known "skeleton" suits include many of the Pearlies' symbols such as hearts (charity), horseshoes (luck), doves, (peace), crosses (faith), and donkey carts or flower pots for the Costers, among other symbols. Pearly Queens are also sometimes known as "donahs". If you want to join the group, however, you'll have to marry into one of the families, as the traditions are hereditary and only stay within the original families that formed from Henry Croft.

Several Pearly groups formed as a result of Croft's charity work, with the first being the Original Pearly Kings and Queens in 1875 and reformed in 1975, including several of the original Pearly titles such as the City of London, Westminster, Victoria, Hackney, Dalston, Tower Hamlets, Shoreditch, Islington, and Horton. The longest continually active organization is the Pearly Guild, which has existed since 1902. Modern Pearly groups include the Pearly Kings and Queens Guild, which formed in 2001. Each organization is tied to a church in central London and coordinates its charity work with these institutions.

25 FAMOUS COCKNEYS AND EASTENDERS

The East End of London has always been a hotbed of creativity, culture, and characters. From iconic actors and musicians to legendary gangsters, the area has produced some of the most famous and fascinating people in British history. In this article, we take a look at the 25 most famous Cockneys and East Londoners, from David Beckham and Michael Caine to the Kray twins and Amy Winehouse. Whether you're a Londoner yourself or just a fan of the city's rich cultural heritage, there's something here for everyone. So, without further ado, let's dive in and discover the stories of these legendary East Enders.

Note: some may argue that a few of these figures are not 'true' Eastenders or Cockneys. Identity like this is fluid – it's not just where you were born, or the accent you speak, but also what class you are and how you behave. Some may simply be 'honorary' Eastenders. Some may be pretenders, speaking with a Cockney accent because it is advantageous. Your mileage may vary.

1. **David Beckham** was born and raised in Leytonstone, East London. He is a retired professional footballer and is considered one of the greatest players of his generation.

2. **Michael Caine** - Born in Rotherhithe, South East London. He is an Academy Award-winning actor known for his roles in films like The Dark Knight and The Italian Job.

3. **Barbara Windsor** - Born in Shoreditch, East London. She was an actress best known for her role in the Carry-On films and as Peggy Mitchell

in EastEnders.

4. **Ray Winstone** - Born in Hackney, East London. He is an actor known for his roles in films like Sexy Beast and The Departed.

5. **Danny Dyer** - Born in Canning Town, East London. He is an actor and presenter best known for his roles in films like The Football Factory and on TV shows like EastEnders.

6. **Idris Elba** - Born in Hackney, East London. He is an actor known for his roles in TV shows like The Wire and Luther, as well as films like Mandela: Long Walk to Freedom.

7. **Adele** - Born in Tottenham, North London. She is a singer-songwriter known for hits like "Hello" and "Someone Like You".

8. **David Essex** - Born in Plaistow, East London. He is a singer, songwriter, and actor known for his hits like "Rock On" and his role in the film That'll Be the Day.

9. **Bob Hoskins** - Born in Bury St Edmunds but grew up in Finsbury Park, North London. He was an actor

known for his roles in films like Who Framed Roger Rabbit and Mona Lisa.

10. **Jamie Oliver** - Born in Clavering, Essex. He is a chef and restaurateur known for his TV shows and cookbooks.

11. **Vinnie Jones** - Born in Watford but grew up in Hertfordshire and later moved to London. He is a former professional footballer turned actor known for his roles in films like Snatch and Lock, Stock, and Two Smoking Barrels.

12. **Lennox Lewis** - Born in West Ham, East London. He is a retired professional boxer and former undisputed heavyweight champion of the world.

13. **Paloma Faith** - Born in Hackney, East London. She is a singer-songwriter known for hits like "Only Love Can Hurt Like This" and "Picking Up the Pieces."

14. **Steve McQueen** - Born in London. He is a film director known for his work on films like 12 Years a Slave and Shame.

15. **Alfred Hitchcock** - Born in Leytonstone, East London. He was a film director known for his work on films like Psycho and Rear Window.

16. **Jack the Ripper** - An unidentified serial killer who operated in Whitechapel, East London, in 1888.

17. **Amy Winehouse** - Born in Southgate, North London. She was a singer-songwriter known for her hits like "Rehab" and "Back to Black."

18. **Lenny McLean** - Born in Hoxton, East London. He was a bare-knuckle boxer, actor, and author known for his autobiography The Guv'nor.

19. **Boy George** - Born in Eltham, South East London. He is a singer-songwriter and DJ known for his work with Culture Club.

20. **Mary Berry** was born in Bath but moved to London as a child. She is a cook, author, and TV presenter known for her work on The Great British Bake Off.

21. **Peter Sellers** - Born in Southsea but raised in South East London. He was an actor known for his roles in

films like The Pink Panther and Dr. Strangelove.

22. **Paul Gascoigne** - Born in Gateshead, but later played for Tottenham Hotspur and Lazio. He is a retired professional footballer known for his skill and controversial behavior.

23. **Ronnie Kray** - Born in Hoxton, East London. He was a notorious gangster and one-half of the Kray twins, who were involved in organized crime in the 1960s.

24. **Phil Collins** was born in Chiswick, West London. He is a singer-songwriter and drummer known for his work with Genesis and his solo career.

25. **East Enders** is a fictional TV soap opera set in the East End of London that has been on the air since 1985.

40 LONDON SLANG PHRASES AND THEIR HISTORIES

Cockney rhyming slang, a distinct language primarily used in the East End of London, has been in existence since the 19th Century. There are debates about its origins, with some suggesting it was a simple shorthand used by market vendors, while others believe it was a code to conceal criminal activity. Regardless of its beginnings, rhyming slang has become an integral part of Cockney culture and identity. If you're struggling to understand the words and phrases associated with this unique London language, we've compiled a list of ten common Cockney rhyming slang phrases and their meanings below.

Apples and Pears

"Apples and Pears" is a rhyme for "steps and stairs." In the days of the costermongers (market stall owners) in the early 19th Century, the stall owners often had their fruits and vegetables on gradations for display. This display style was also called "steps and stairs," and the rhyme became synonymous with the goods themselves.

Pig's Ear

Certainly not a literal pig's ear; this is a rhyming slang way of saying "beer." This was originally a much longer rhyming phrase, "tiddly wink of pig's ear," which meant "drink of beer." There's no real reason for this beyond being a good rhyme (as is the case with most Cockney slang), and there are several other rhyming words and phrases for beer.

Box of Toys

A "box of toys" is another way of saying noise. The origin is owed to a box of toys making a loud noise when kids are going through them looking for the toy they want most.

Trouble and Strife

This is a rhyming phrase that might get a lot of husbands in trouble if their partners heard it because it is a rhyme for one's wife. It's not hard to figure out how this one got started since some husbands tend to consider their spouses as the source of a lot of their grief (though it's usually self-inflicted).

Pie and Mash

"Pie and Mash" as a phrase simply refers to money as it rhymes with "cash." It also has a much cruder meaning in that it also rhymes with "slash," which is a much more vulgar way of saying "urinate," so be careful to note how it's being used.

Dicky/Dickie

Dicky is one of those Cockney terms that's a shortened form of a loner phrase. Dicky is short for "dicky bird," which around the 1700s meant any small bird common in the UK, like a sparrow or chickadee. By the time Cockney rhyming slang came around a century later, they used the "bird" as a rhyme for "word." Telling someone, "You've got my dicky" is the same as making a promise.

Cobblers Awls

This phrase is a bit more blue-collar and is a rhyme for "balls." A similar English slang term is "bollocks," which tends to be used for calling out a lie (ala, "That's a load of bollocks"). Cobblers awls are used in the same way and often shortened to simply "cobblers."

Rosie Lee

If someone offers you a cuppa Rosie Lee, it would be good manners to take it. This is because Rosie Lee is a rhyming slang phrase for tea. The phrase first appeared in print in 1925 and is sometimes shortened to simply "Rosie."

Barcardi Breezer

This is a phrase that can have a couple of meanings based on its rhyme. One is a substitute for "geezer" (a very old person), and the other can describe their freezer. It just goes to show that sometimes you really have to pay attention to the context in which Cockney is using the slang.

Crowded Space

This is a rhyme referring to a suitcase, which can sometimes be pretty crowded depending on how many things you pack into it for a trip.

North and South

If you're ever told to shut your north and south, that's because it rhymes with mouth. This phrase can have more positive uses, but a fair amount of the time, it's used on people who are talking too much, bragging, or getting way ahead of themselves.

Tom Cruise

Cockneys aren't talking about the movie star when they refer to a Tom Cruise; they are actually referring to a bruise, given the real Tom Cruise's penchant for doing his own stunts and seriously injuring himself in the process (such as when he broke his leg filming Mission Impossible: Fallout), his name not only rhymes well with bruise but is quite appropriate.

Barney Rubble

Fans of the Oceans movie trilogy might recognize this phrase as used by Mockney Don Cheadle's character, Basher Tarr. Far from referring to Fred Flintstone's co-worker and best buddy, Barney Rubble is a rhyme for "trouble." Normally, Cockneys will leave off the surname and just say something like, "Well, that looks like Barney."

King Dick

King Dick is not as bad of an insult as Americans might think, but it's still certainly an insult. King Dick is a rhyme for another British insult: "thick." Thick normally means someone who isn't very smart or is particularly dense. If you're being called a King Dick, it means someone thinks you're dumb.

Mickey Mouse

Oh, boy! Naturally, no Cockney is actually referring to Disney's most famous character when they say "Mickey Mouse" or shorten it to "Mickey." In Cockney rhyming slang, this means "house," though "Taking the Mickey" in English slang is similar to "taking the piss," which means to mock someone or something.

Adam and Eve

Adam and Eve can have two different meanings in Cockney rhyming slang, neither of which are Biblical. The first and most common is "believe," as in "I can't believe Adam and Eve."

The other meaning is "leave," which can be either just going or having to beat a hasty departure. The first originated as far back as the late 19th Century, while the second came about around the 1930s.

April Showers

If you remember the old phrase "April showers bring May flowers," you're not far off from the meaning of this Cockney phrase. April showers is a shorthand way of saying flowers and sometimes you can shorten it to say "I got my girl some Aprils for Valentine's Day."

Dog and Bone

A Cockney rhyming slang phrase is a simple rhyme that means "telephone."

Half-inch

This phrase came about in the 1920s and is a rhyme for "pinch." Of course, this doesn't mean a pinch like most of us would think, but pinch is itself a slang term for meaning "steal."

As an example, you might hear someone say, "Oy, my wallet's been half-inched!"

Didgeridoo

It has nothing to do with the Australian musical instrument, "didgeridoo," in this case, is simple rhyming slang for "clue," as in "I haven't got a didgeridoo where your keys got off to." This doesn't really have a discernable origin and appears to be another rhyme that came about because it sounded similar.

Bees & Honey

This rhyming phrase is a stand-in for money. Bees are seen as hard workers, and their work produces honey, so humans' hard work produces money. You'll definitely need some bees and honey if you want to hit the pub tonight.

Can't Keep Still

"Can't keep still" rhymes with treadmill, which, back in the 19th Century, was a form of criminal punishment. It started off having no other purpose than to keep prisoners active, though it eventually came to be used to power prison mills and pumps. Today, it refers more to exercise machines instead of these.

Coals & Coke

Anytime something stops working, it can be said that it's "coals and coke" or "broke." In the past, coal and coke (a porous coal-based fuel) came in large blocks and had to be broken down in order to be used as fuel.

Dental Flosser

Cockney is full of colorful phrases that can be used to insult others, and "dental flosser" is one of them. The phrase rhymes with "tosser," so it has nothing to do with the health of someone's teeth, but that the Cockney views that person as a jerk.

Elephant's Trunk

Another colorful epithet courtesy of the Cockneys, "elephant's trunk," is a Cockney way of saying that someone is drunk. Besides the clear rhyme, if you've ever seen an elephant's trunk swaying, you may recognize the same motion of someone too drunk to walk a straight line.

Jack/Jack Jones

It's not exactly a perfect rhyme, but in Cockney slang, "Jack," shortened from "Jack Jones," means to be alone. The origin is from an 1890s music hall song, "'E Dunno Where 'E Are," about a man named Jack Jones who came into some money and thought he was better than his coworkers, an attitude that left him alone. Another use of this phrase is "on my Jack," which means "on my own."

Lionels/Lionel Blairs

"Lionels" or "Lionel Blairs" is a reference to bell-bottom pants or "flares" because of how they flare out at the bottom. The phrase has its origins in real-life Canadian-born dancer and television presenter Lionel Blair, who we can assume wore those pants in the 70s like most people, though it's more likely that his name is just a convenient rhyme.

Radio Rental

"Radio rental" is a rhyme for "mental." If a Cockney thinks you might have a screw loose, they could refer to you as being a "bit radio rental."

Stand to Attention

This is a Cockney rhyming phrase that has a certain respectability to it. "Stand to attention" rhymes with pension and has its origins in the pensioners at the Royal Chelsea Hospital, a retirement home for veterans of the British Army. "Standing to attention" is something that a soldier is expected to do in formation.

Weep & Wail

You might have heard this phrase used by Lin-Manuel Miranda in the film Mary Poppins Returns during the song "Trip a Little Light Fantastic." If you didn't understand it from the song lyrics, a "weep and wail" rhymes with tale, and it means to tell your story.

"Allow It"

In a previous article on London slang, we covered the word "Roadman," and it's from these knowledgeable neighbors that a lot of London slang originates. "Allow it" is one such phrase. It's pronounced with the "a" and actually means the opposite, asking someone to leave off or stop.

Angel

Of course, with this term, we're not talking about heavenly beings but one of the city's many vibrant neighborhoods. When people start talking about "Angel" in a non-religious sense, they're referring to the inner part of London that comprises transport fare zone 1. Zone 1 covers roughly the same area as the Underground's Circle Line and includes Tube stations such as Earl's Court, Baker Street, Covent Garden, Elephant & Castle, and Angel.

"Boris Bikes"

Introduced during the mayorship of Boris Johnson, this term refers to the bicycles available for hire across London. Even though the previous mayor, Ken Livingstone, was the one who proposed the scheme and got it passed, the cycles didn't come out until Johnson was in office, and, being a keen cycling enthusiast himself, he got tagged with the nickname for the bikes. Not sure how many people call them that since he hasn't been mayor for quite some time and his prime ministership was a disaster.

Bruv

You've probably heard this one if you have watched the Kingsman films or Attack the Block. "Bruv" is a street slang term that is short for "brother" and is typically used to refer to one's mates. It started as a Cockney pronunciation of "brother" (or "bruvver") that got shortened.

China

And speaking of Cockneys, if you find yourself in East London, you might hear an older Cockney refer to someone as "me old China." This originates with Cockney rhyming slang in which "China plate" means "me old mate."

"The City"

If you're familiar with the various boroughs in London and how the city's government is organized, you know that London is largely broken down into Greater London and the City of London. When you hear people talk about "the City," they are most likely referring to the latter, which has its own separate government (the City of London Corporation) and Lord Mayor.

Inspector Sands

The term "Inspector Sands" comes from the London Underground and is code that you hopefully won't hear over the announcement system as it is a notice to Tube workers that there is a fire. The idea is that the term is less likely to cause panic, though at this point, most people who hear it know what it means anyway.

"The Knowledge"

If you take one of London's famous Black Cabs, you can be certain your driver knows the streets of the city like the back of his own hand. "The Knowledge" refers to the comprehensive test that Black Cab drivers have to pass to be allowed to have a license. Black Cabbies have to learn over 25,000 streets and 320 routes, as well as memorize 20,000 different landmarks. Cabbies will literally study for years, and the first-time pass rate for the exam is roughly 10%.

Walkie Talkie

Since we all have mobile phones now, no one is actually referring to old communication devices. "Walkie Talkie" is the nickname for the skyscraper at 20 Fenchurch Street, which looks exactly like the old walkie-talkies that police officers used to carry. London has plenty of creative nicknames for its skyscrapers, such as "The Gherkin" for 30 St. Mary Axe and "The Cheesegrater" for 122 Leadenhall Street.

From Ends

"From Ends" is another way of identifying yourself as a local or someone who's "from the area."

LONDON STREET SLANG

English is a forever-evolving language. It changes the most on the streets of London as the various ethnicities that have settled in London co-mingle their native languages with English. Interesting things result from this. There are new words all the time, old words are brought back into fashion, and some words now mean the opposite of what they used to mean. It's all very fascinating and confusing to visitors as well!

Here are a few more new words that have made their way into the current London Urban vernacular. Some of them may still have you scratching your head. And the meaning may completely change by tomorrow morning!

Peng – N – Excellent, very good, attractive. Popularized on the streets of London in the ethnic neighborhoods. "She is so Peng." "Or that food was the Pengest munch."

Peak – Adj – One would think this would be an adjective to describe something grand, but it actually means the exact opposite. "There's a rail strike again this weekend; it's such a peak."

Bossman – N – Used to refer to a shop owner or someone working in the service industry. Like the person serving you chicken at the local chippie. "'Ello Bossman, I'll have four thighs."

Mandem – N – A group of acquaintances that aren't as cool as they think, slightly ropey. "Oh, looks like the mandem are hanging out at the skate park again."

Roadman – N – That intimidating, slightly

sketchy-looking character who knows the neighborhood better than anyone. Probably the person to ask for directions. "What? Does he think he's some kind of roadman?"

Northerner – N – Anyone who lives outside the M25 ring road that surrounds London. "I think he's a Northerner."

Blower – N – The phone. "Hey mate, your dad's on the blower."

Lit – Adj – Something that is exciting or a big bash. "Man, that party was lit!"

Dench – Adj – Someone who has bulked themselves up successfully. "You are so dench now that you have been down the gym."

Wavey – Adj – To be drunk or high on drugs. "He was so wavey at the party last night."
In Ends – N – Your local area. "I've been in ends all day, mate."

Link – V – To meet up with friends or hang out. "Don't forget to link up with us later."

Chirpsing – *V* – Casual flirting. "He was over there chirpsing with the girls."

Choong – *N* – Good looking, attractive. "Oh man, he was soooo choong."

Tekker – *N* – Someone with great technical ability. "Hey, take this over to the tekkers down the street to get it fixed."

Vex – *Adj* – Angry. "I heard her on the phone earlier; she was vex."

Reh teh teh – *Adj* – A phrase that basically means etc.

Looking criss – *Adj* – Looking fresh, sharp. "I saw her coming out of the hairdresser, and she was looking cross."

Kicks – *N* – A pair of American-style sneakers (normally called trainers in England). "Did you see his beautiful new kicks?"

LONDON LINGO

One thing you'll notice when you travel to London is all the strange words they use to describe things. Sometimes, they make sense; sometimes, they don't.

Now, there will be some words used elsewhere, but I tried to capture words that, when I hear them, make me think of London. So, here's your guide to some useful London Lingo or, as I like to just say, London Words.

- **Tube** = London Underground Network
- **The Knowledge** = The cumulative knowledge of London's black cab drivers that they have to learn to be licensed. They have to learn every street in London.
- **Boris Bus** = Boris Johnson's key platform for replacing the old London Routemaster bus.
- **Red Ken** = The name of London's former Mayor Ken Livingston, who leaned VERY far to the left.
- **The Standard** = What some call the Evening Standard – the evening paper dedicated to London.
- **The City** = The City of London – the square mile bit of central London that goes back 2 thousand years.
- **Square Mile** = The City of London also
- **Congestion Charge** = Tax on all cars entering the central London congestion charge zone.
- **Silicon Roundabout** = Area around Old Street that's a hub for new media and tech companies.

- **Council Estate** = Public housing
- **The Blitz** = Period in 1940 when London was bombed by the Nazis
- **M25** = The Orbital Highway that encircles London
- **Westway** = Elevated Highway in West London
- **Mind the Gap** = Watch your step when stepping from a train to a platform.
- **The Palace** = When someone says the Palace, they're almost always referring to Buckingham Palace, the Queen's official residence in London.
- **Buck House** = Buckingham Palace
- The Tower = Tower of London
- **A to Z** = A popular London map guide that's indispensable to locals and long-term visitors (extra note – Londoners will say 'A to Zed').
- **GMT** = Greenwich Mean Time
- **Cockney** = Someone born within earshot of the bells of St Mary-le-Bow
- **Offy** = Convenience Store that sells alcohol
- **Off License** = Convenience Store that sells alcohol

- **Take Away** = Cheap to-go food.
- **Crossrail** = New cross London underground railway line currently under construction.
- **Bobby** = London Policeman
- **Clip Joint** = A club that claims to be a strip club but usually comes with £100 bottles of water. Avoid.
- **Zebra Crossing** = Pedestrian crossing.
- **Home Counties** = Generic name for the counties around London, which are Bedfordshire, Berkshire, Buckinghamshire, Cambridgeshire, Dorset, Essex, Hampshire, Hertfordshire, Kent, Middlesex, Oxfordshire, Surrey, and Sussex.
- **Nappy Valley** = Areas of London with high birthrates like Battersea.

COCKNEY SLANG DICTIONARY

A

Adam and Eve – believe

Able and Willing - Shilling

Adam and son –– done

Alan Minter - printer or splinter

Alan Whickers – knickers

Alex Nash - slash (urinate)

Almond Rocks –– "Socks"

Apple pip - dip

Apples and pears – stairs

Aris (short for Aristotle) –– bottle

Artful Dodger – lodger

Arthur Conan Doyle - boil

Arthur J. Rank –– wank ('I was just having an
Arthur J.')

Ascot Races – braces

Atilla the Hun - 2:1 degree

Aunt Joanna – piano

B

Baa lamb - tram
Baked Bean – Queen
Baker's Dozen – Cousin
Ball and Chalk – Walk
Barclays Bank, J. Arthur Rank, Jodrell Bank,
Barnaby Rudge – Judge
Barnet Fair – hair
Barney Rubble – trouble
Basil Brush - thrush
Battlecruiser – boozer
Bees and honey – money
Berk (short for [[Berkshire Hunt]]) — cunt
(metaphorical — referring to person, not
genitalia)
Betty Boo/ Eartha Kitt - poo
Bill Oddie - voddie (vodka)
Billie Piper - windscreen wiper
Billy (short for billy-goat) - coat
Billy Ray Cyrus - virus
Bird (short for bird lime) — time (in prison)
Bird lime – time (in prison)
Black cabs — "
Boat Race – face
Bob Hope – soap

Boracic lint - broke, skint
Bottle (short for bottle and glass) — arse (audacity)
Bottle and glass – arse
Brad Pitt - Brad Pitt means fit
Brahms and Liszt – pissed (drunk)
Brass Tacks – facts
Bread and Cheese – sneeze
Bread and Honey – money
Bricks and Mortar – daughter
Bristol (short for Bristol City, a football team) — titty (breast) (usually plural)
Bristol City – breasts
Britney Spears - ears, tears, or beers
Brown Bread – dead
brown bread — dead
Bubble (short for bubble bath) — laugh (noun)
Bubble and Squeak – Greek
Bubble Bath – Laugh
Butcher's (short for butcher's hook) — look (noun)
Butcher's hook – a look

C

Cadbury's Flake — mistake
Cattle trucked — fucked (meaning
exhausted, f.e. 'I feel cattle trucked')
Chalfont St. Giles – piles
chalk (short for Chalk Farm) — arm
Chalk Farm – arm
Charlie Drake - steak
Cheese and kisses - Mrs
Cheese and kisses — missus (wife or
girlfriend)
Cheesy Quaver - favor
Cherry Ripe — "Pipe"
Cherry tart — heart
Cherry-og — "Dog"
China plate – mate (friend)
Chocolate flaked — "baked"
City slickers — knickers
Coat hanger - clanger, mistake
cobblers (short for cobbler's awls) — balls
(testicles)
Cock and Hen – ten
Cocoa — say so, as in "I should cocoa."
Cows and Kisses – Missus (wife)
Cream-crackered — knackered (slang word

meaning tired)

Cuff link - drink (alcoholic)

Cup of John — "cup of coffee" (John coffee)

Cuppa, sausage and a slice - nice

Currant bun – sun (also The Sun, a British newspaper)

Custard and jelly – telly (television)

Custard Creme — "dream"

Cuts and scratches — "matches"

D

Daisy dancers - stairs

Daisy Roots – boots

Damien Hirst - first class degree

Darby and Joan – moan

Dickie Dirt — "shirt"

Dicky bird – word

Dicky Dirt – shirt

Diet Coke - joke

Dinky Doos – shoes

Dog and bone – phone

Dog's meat – feet [from early 20th c.]

Donald Trump - hump

Duck and Dive – skive

Duke of Kent — rent ("The landlord's

putting up the duke.")
Duncan Goodhew - clue
Dustbin lid – kid
Dusty bin and supersonic — gin and tonic

E

Elephant's Trunk – drunk

F

Finsbury (short for Finsbury Park) —
arc(light) (in theatres)
Direman's hose - nose
Flowery Dell – cell
Dour by two — Jew
Frazer-Nash — slash (urinate)
French egg - enough (un ouef)
Frog and Toad – road

G

Gamma ray - stray
Gareth Hunt — cunt (most common at the

height of the actor's fame)
Gary Glitter — shitter
German bands — "hands"
German beer/ ginger beer - engineer
Ginger (short for ginger beer), Brighton Pier
— queer (homosexual)
Ginger hair — "bear"
Godforsaken - bacon
Gordon Brown - clown
Grass in the park — "nark" (informer)
Gregory Peck — neck
Grumble and grunt — cunt
Gypsy's kiss – piss

H

Half-inch – pinch (to steal)
Hampsteads (short for Hampstead Heath)
— teeth
Hampton Wick – prick
Hank Marvin – starving
Harry Hill - pill, birth control
Harry Randall — Candle
Hearts of oak — "broke" (no money)
Holy Ghost — toast
Holy Grail - email

Hovis - dead (from brown bread)

I

Ian Beale - real
In and out — snout
Irish pig – wig
Iron hoof — poof (homosexual)
Isle of Wight – tights
Itchy ring - Burger King

J

Jabba the Hutt - shut
Jack Jones — own (as in 'on your own')
Jam-jar – car
James Blunt — cunt (derogatory)
Jayme Gibbs
Jet fighter - all-nighter
Jimmy Riddle – piddle
Joanna – piano (pronounced 'pianna' in Cockney)

K

Kangaroo pouch - couch
Kettle — Watch (kettle and hob, fob (watch))
Khyber Pass – arse
Kick and Prance – dance
King Lear — Ear
KY Jelly - telly

L

Lady Godiva – fiver
Lager and lime - spine
Laugh and joke — "smoke"
Laugh n a joke – smoke
Lionel Blairs – flares
Lisa Tarbucks - Starbucks
Loaf of Bread – head
Longer and lingers — "fingers"
Loop the loop – soup
Lump of lead - head

M

Malcom X - text
Merlyn Rees - piece, lunch
Mickey Bliss - piss (taking the Mickey)
Mike and dave — microwave (CJ)
Mince Pies – eyes
Minces (short for mince pies) — eyes
Mork and Mindy – windy'
Mutt and Jeff — deaf

N

Nelly (short for Nelly Duff) — puff (life, as
used in the phrase "Not on your nelly!")
Nervous tick — dick
Night Boat to Cairo - giro
Noddy holders - shoulders
North and south – mouth

O

Obi Wan Kenobi - mobile phone
Oily rag - fag (cigarette)

Oliver Twist — pissed (drunk)

Ones and twos — shoes

Orchestra stalls – balls

Oxford (short for Oxford scholar) — dollar
(five shilling piece, since Royal Mint made
dollar coins with 'Dollar and Five Shillings
on them, until decimalization)

P

Pat and Mick – sick

Peckham Rye – tie

Pen and ink — stink (noun)

Perpetual loser - boozer

Pete Tong — wrong (as in "it's all gone a bit
Pete Tong")

Pig's Ear — "beer"

Pineapple chunk - bunk bed

Pipe your eye — "cry"

Plates of meat – feet

Pony and Trap – crap

Porker, porky (short for pork pie) — lie
(untruth)

R

Rabbit (short for rabbit and pork) — talk
Raspberry (short for raspberry tart) — fart
Raspberry ripple – nipple
Raspberry tart – fart
Rats and Mice – Dice (gambling)
Ricky Gervais - face
Rifles (short for rifle ranges) — changes
Roast Pork – fork
Rock of Ages - wages
Rosie (short for Rosy Lee) — tea
Rosy Lee – tea (drink)
Rub-a-Dub – pub
Ruby Murray – curry

S

Salmon and trout — snout (tobacco)
Sausage and mash — cash
Sausage Roll – goal
Scarper (short for Scapa Flow) — go
Scooby (short for Scooby Doo) — clue
(inkling, as in "I haven't got a scooby.")
Scotch eggs — "legs"

Septic tank – Yank
Sexton Blake — "fake"
Sherbert (short for sherbert dab) – cab
(taxi)
Shirt and tie — "cry"
Skin and Blister – sister
Sky Rocket – pocket
Sparkly clean — "bean"
Strides 'round the houses – trousers
Struggle and grunt — cunt
Sweeney Todd – flying squad
Syrup (short for syrup of figs) — wig (sic)

T

Tables and chairs – stairs
Taters (short for potatoes in the mould) —
cold (adjective)
Tea leaf – thief
Thruppennies (short for thruppeny bits) —
"tits"
Tid (short for tiddlywink) — Chink
(Chinese person)
Tilburys (short for Tilbury docks) - pox
(venereal disease)
Titfer (short for tit-for-tat) — hat

Tom and Dick – sick
Tom tit – shit
Tomfoolery – jewellery
Tommy Tank — wank
Tommy guns - the runs (diarrhea)
Tommy Trinder – window
Town halls — balls (testicles)
Trouble and strife – wife
Turtle doves — gloves
Two and eight – state (of upset)

U

Uncle Ned — "bed"

V

Vera & Philharmonic — gin and tonic
Vera Lynn - gin
Vera Lynn - skins

W

Weasel and Stoat — "Coat"

Weeping Willow — "Pillow"
Whistle and flute – suit (of clothes)
Wonga – cash